Stan & Jan Berenstain's "IT'S ALL IN THE FAMILY"

D1616792

BALLANTINE BOOKS · NEW YORK

Presenting Your Favorite Funny Family of All Time!

See:

- the fat father flunk the pinch test
- the gutsy mother make a jock of herself
- the three kids freak out on monsters

  ...pig out on wild blackberries

  ...get straight A's in Sex Ed

  ...spoil the dog rotten

  ...make the cat crazy

- and lots, lots more!

DAD'S DIET

OVERWEIGHT?
TRY THE
PINCH
TEST

"OUCH!"

"I've solved your problem, Dad! There are four things in here that don't have any calories at all— water, coffee, tea and mushrooms!"

"It's really quite simple—Daddy doesn't want you to go jogging with him because he doesn't want to look foolish."

(DAD'S DIET)

"He's opening the fridge...he's reading the sign...."

"Oh, stop feeling so sorry for yourself!"

*"No, you didn't hear thunder—
just my stomach rumbling."*

"OUCH!"

MOM
WORKS
OUT

*"I'm glad you're favorably impressed,
because I just signed up for the whole course."*

"Boy, Mom really can shake it, can't she?"

"Dad's is bigger, but Mom's is harder."

"What a workout—thirty minutes of aerobics, three sets of paddleball, and then ten laps around the indoor track!"

"It's for you—one of your jock friends."

"Look, somebody's got to maintain
the sedentary lifestyle or it will be
lost to mankind forever!"

"Dad won! Dad won!"

NEW SCHOOL YEAR

"Now look, Ethel, you stuck me with PTA Mimeograph Chairman <u>last</u> year, and if you think for one minute...."

"Sesame Street it's not."

"Insurance form, third-grade cake sale notice, envelope for PTA dues, back-to-school-night announcement...."

(NEW SCHOOL YEAR)

"Then, if you decide to keep it, the rental goes toward the purchase price."

"I hate to rush you, dear, but this table is scheduled for homework at 6:15 sharp."

"Mom, how's this strike you—instead of the whole committee going home and then coming back after dinner...."

"Wow! Are we gonna get to eat out every time Mom has a PTA meeting?"

SEX ED

"Dad just heard about the Sex Ed unit we're having at school and he's doing an Archie Bunker."

"But she's not always going to <u>be</u> your little girl. Some day she's going to be somebody's <u>big</u> girl."

"It seems like only yesterday that Big Bird and the Cookie Monster were what it was all about."

"It's all so clinical! What about the magic, the romance, the sense of mystery...?"

"Dear, if you just wouldn't take it all so personally!"

"Congratulations...I _think_."

"That was just Unit One—Unit Two goes into Birth control, VD, Premarital Sex...."

SHAPING UP POOCHIE

"Then it's settled—we're going to stop spoiling her and start treating her a little more like a dog!"

"It seems to me, young man, that your dinner is disappearing awfully fast!"

"You said she couldn't sleep with __me__, you didn't say I couldn't sleep with her!"

(SHAPING UP POOCHIE)

"And who, may I ask, let you in?"

"But Dad—she's been on table scraps for seven years. You can't expect her to quit cold turkey."

"It's a classic case of canine nervous breakdown. Has she been under any particular strain lately?"

"She's going to be fine. The vet prescribed plenty of treats and lots of Tender Loving Care."

DISCOUNT STORE

"Honey, this looks like the big league—are you sure you can handle it?"

"Pinch me."

"When he wants to wear my name
on his backside, I'll consider
returning the favor. Until then—"

(DISCOUNT STORE)

"It's not what I went in with, but how do you like it?"

"Please, Ma! All the kids have them! Our teacher even has a special rule for them. We don't 'show and tell,' we just 'tell....'"

*"LOST HUSBAND AND FATHER
NEEDS TO BE PICKED UP AT THE
CHECKOUT COUNTER!"*

*"Or look at it this way—with the
money we saved, we could have a
lovely sit-down dinner at Antoine's."*

OBEDIENCE SCHOOL

"Are you thinking what I'm thinking?"

"This must be the place!"

*"First, may I introduce myself—
KEEP THAT COCKER QUIET!—I'm
Captain Willowby, your instructor
for the next seven weeks. THAT
POODLE'S CHEWING HIS LEASH!..."*

(OBEDIENCE SCHOOL)

"If, on the other hand, the dog does not obey the command...."

"You're doing quite well with your tests, but there's still one problem you're going to have to work on."

"She's doing so well we ought to enter her in the advanced class."

"Now all we have to do is see that she doesn't backslide."

VALENTINES

"*Gee, Dad, a couple of bucks won't do it!*
Valentines have gone through the roof—just like everything else!"

"For Mom? It's your funeral!"

"Why not? I'm an adult!"

(VALENTINES)

"It must be serious. He blew his whole allowance on one oversized Valentine that takes extra postage."

"Boy, if I'd known how great I was going to do, I wouldn't have sent myself all those 'Guess Who's' for insurance!"

"Don't take it so hard, Son. Most men would give their eye teeth to be attractive to women."

"Nice going, Pop. You really knocked her socks off."

THE MATING-GAME

"Now, look, it's about time the children learned a little something about the facts of life—and since Poochie's in season anyway...."

"But, Poochie, Rex Prince of Chadburn will make a wonderful daddy for your puppies!"

"Here it is, right here in my Sex Ed book—Gestation Period in Canines...."'

(THE MATING-GAME)

"...and listen to this—'On its reproductive journey a single male cell travels a distance equivalent to 17 earth orbits!"

"...three, four, five... six, seven...eight..."

NO TV FOR A WEEK

"You know how you're always complaining about too much television? Well, their whole school just voted to swear off for a week!"

"So far so good— except for Poochie."

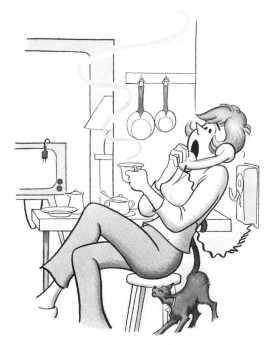

"I tell you, it's rough. Without my Phil Donahue fix in the morning, I'm just no good."

(NO TV FOR A WEEK)

"How do you expect us to do our
homework without TV?
We can't concentrate!"

"Mommy! Daddy's sneaking a
look at The Newlywed Game!"

*"Well, I suppose it's working.
They are getting to know each
other better."*

*"Longest week of
my life."*

MONSTER PARTY

"*Why don't you just have a Come-As-You-Are Party? I've seen most of your friends.*"

"How's he going to pick out a mask if he's afraid to go into the store?"

"I warned him not to look in the mirror."

(MONSTER PARTY)

"Yuck! The pumpkin's insides
are scarier than the pumpkin!"

"It's like Pin the Tail on the
Donkey, except that instead of a
tail and a donkey...."

"Relax. It's just a group of daddies come to pick up their little monsters."

"Sure, jump in—we're having a special tonight on nightmares."

"I don't know if I like the idea of my daughter playing a guy's game."

"I just showed him an article about the growing availability of college scholarships for female athletes."

(BASKETBALL STAR)

"I think I made a believer out of Dad. I just beat his butt in a little one-on-one."

"Meet Mary Louise Cooper, our center."

"Uh-oh, I think our side is in big trouble."

"My daddy!"

THANKSGIVING PLAY

"Boy, have I got something to be thankful for—I beat out Lou Ann Schmidt for the best part in the Thanksgiving play!"

"Now, sweetie, it's a perfectly beautiful costume—and after we take a little tuck here and there...."

"I can't hear you, Indian!...I can't hear you, Turkey Gobbler!...I can't hear you, Pilgrim Maiden!"

(THANKSGIVING PLAY)

"How-I-am-great-chief-I-bring-you-maize."

"Now, I'm not going to warn you wheat shucks again!"

"'Gobble, gobble, gobble!...
Gobble, gobble, gobble!'"

*"What **I'm** most thankful for is*
that we got through that crummy play!"

GARAGE
SALE

"Now, this is how I want the ad to read: 'No more room...
must sacrifice fabulous household goods.'..."

*"We could just get a truck and
haul it all over to the dump."*

*"You mean you actually expect
people to come and buy
this junk?"*

(GARAGE SALE)

"ALL MERCHANDISE PRICED AS MARKED!...ALL SALES FINAL!..."

"Would you believe—our sixth sale today?"

"Come quick! A couple of them got into the house!"

"Seventy-eight dollars and twenty-two cents _clear profit!_"

SCHOOL FAIR

"You better do what he says, Dad—it's Mr. Bensonmeyer, the principal!"

"Now, these tickets have to last you all afternoon—is that understood? I SAID—IS THAT UNDERSTOOD?"

"...wealth, travel, a long life and a very poor report card if you don't pull up your socks in Social Studies and Math."

(SCHOOL FAIR)

"Here's your lunch, Mom!"

"What's the matter, Mom
—don't you know us?"

"Dad's feeling a little better now. It was either the Loop-O-Plane or the pepperoni pizza."

"It might be a lot simpler if they just raised school taxes."

THEME PARK

"There's no way of seeing everything so let's choose a few high spots...."

"Don't worry! He's just a great big p-p-pussycat."

"We pay five bucks a head to ride around in the blazing sun with the windows rolled up and we call _them_ baboons."

(THEME PARK)

"I gotta admit it—Daddy surprised me going on The Big Ride!"

"This was the <u>slanty room</u> Daddy was warning us about."

"All I said was it looks kind of interesting."

"I said, 'We'll see!'"

CABIN AT THE LAKE

"Oh boy! Just like the 'Wilderness Family!'"

"A-a-ah! Can't you just feel
yourself unwinding?"

"All right, so a little frog came
out of the pump. He's probably
cleaner than you are."

(CABIN AT THE LAKE)

"How's the bottom—
firm or yucky?"

"Five quarts of wild blackberries!
I'll be able to put up enough jam for
half our Christmas list!"

"Mother, if you don't take your turn, you're going to lose all your hotels!"

"Look—if you weren't having a good time, why didn't you just say so?"

"Remember, now—we're looking for basic economic transportation."

"Well, what do you think?"

"My mechanic doesn't think
your old car's worth much—
but you look like such a
nice family...."

(NEW CAR)

"—dealer prep, destination charges, title cost, local taxes and state taxes—which means I can put you in this little baby for a grand total of...."

"Don't you think twice around the block is enough, dear?"

"But, I just vacuumed!"

"That new-car smell—It's gone!"

FLEA MARKET

"I don't get it—people breaking their necks to spend a fortune on stuff they've been throwing out for years!"

"No—strictly pussycat ashtrays. Been collecting 'em for years. Got 266 of 'em. Had a special room built. You ought to come see 'em. Here's my card."

"Well, maybe that explains why his prices are so competitive."

(FLEA MARKET)

"Oh, Daddy—please!"

"What do you suppose would be
a reasonable offer for a thing like that?"

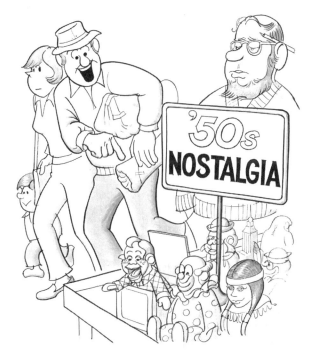

"Look! A genuine Howdy Doody jack-in-the-box—and there's Mr. Bluster, Clarabelle, and Princess Summer-Fall-Winter-Spring!"

"You heard what the man said—'Howdy-Doodiana is an investment!'"

HOME
REPAIRS

"It's something called an 'estimate,' I think he said."

"Yes, I think we can take care of you."

"You never saw that doorstop I made for my mom in woodshop, did you—or the tie rack I made my dad?"

"Here it is: 'Common Mistakes in the Use of the Saber Saw....'"

"Nothing to it, really. It's like running a seam on a sewing machine."

"Now go up to the attic and get all those lamps that don't work."

"Darn good chili!"

MOM POWER

"Welcome to the first meeting of the Committee To Get a Traffic Light at Fifth and Elm."

"Well, I don't want to be negative,
but I've seen catchier acronyms."

"Steady now."

(MOM POWER)

"Look at it this way, Pop—we're not losing a wife and mom, we're gaining a media event."

"Molly Pitcher, Clara Barton, Carry Nation...women have always taken stands on issues."

"Mom's a star!"

"But most of all, I want to thank all the little people...."

KITTY LITTER

"But, Clara, we have a nice, clean maternity box for you."

"She's just a little nervous, Poochie. You remember how you felt when you had your first litter."

"A little j-e-a-l-o-u-s."

(KITTY LITTER)

"You know, I'm not so sure this is the best approach."

"Consider the advantages of a cat as a pet—its independence, its cleanliness, easily housebroken...."

"They're all gone, Poochie...all gone. An old lady on Dittman Street just took the last two."

"The next one around here that gets pregnant is going to have to answer to me!"

COMMUNITY CLEANUP

"This lady made such an eloquent appeal on the subject that I move she be appointed Community Cleanup Chairperson by acclamation!"

"Our mom is chairperson,
so we got our pick of the jobs."

"Now, hold it! If we start trash-
picking the dumper, we're going
to be right back where we
started!"

"How would you like to be married to that?"

"All right—all those <u>not</u> in favor of talking to Mr. Johnson about cleaning up his act, cluck like a chicken."

"Well, there goes the neighborhood!"

"Really, hon, some of that stuff was just too good to throw away."

THE ALLOWANCE HASSLE

"Oh, we've got the basic allowances worked out. Now we're negotiating the inflation factors and the cost-of-living allowances."

"Have you noticed how much more time the decision-making process takes when it's your own money?"

"It's called an IOU, sweetie, and there's absolutely no reason to call the police!"

(THE ALLOWANCE HASSLE)

"Welcome to the club!"

"You know, there's nothing more disgusting than having a filthy-rich little brother."

"This allowance idea just isn't working out—it's turned one of them into a spendthrift, one into a miser, and one into a loan officer."

"Allowances were such a headache, we're trying a new system—it's called 'chores.'"

GREEN THUMB

"How was your day, Sweetie? Mine was absolutely __wonderful!__"

"I thought we might beef up the beds with a little topsoil and peat moss."

"During gardening season Mom is interested in all growing things—except us."

(GREEN
THUMB)

*"Congratulations. You not only got
rid of those pesky aphids, you
developed that long-sought-for
variety—the black rose."*

*"Think of it as a trade-off—the cardinals
are at least as pretty as the honeybells."*

"A word to the wise: If Mom finds out it's you that's eating her begonias, it's you for the p-o-u-n-d."

"You know, if I had had a greenhouse for forcing, I could have taken First."

FOURTH OF JULY PICNIC

"Hey, this looks like a good spot."

"I think you're being a little hard on your brother. I'm sure Billy didn't let his flag touch the ground *intentionally*."

"That's right—in 1776, and then again in 1812. But ever since then we've been pretty good friends."

(FOURTH OF JULY PICNIC)

PICNIC LUNCH
ALL YOU CAN EAT
FOR $5.00
COUNTY ASSOCIATION BENEFIT

"Paper plates wouldn't be such a problem if you weren't determined to make an insufferable pig of yourself."

MOTHERS' SACK RACE
ALL MOMS WELCOME

FLOUR

FEED

FERTILIZER

"For Pete's sake, Honey, if the soldiers at Valley Forge had complained about every hardship, we'd still be a British colony."

"I don't know, Son. But I certainly _hope_ I would have."

"It sort of gets me right here—or maybe it's the piccalilli I had for lunch."

"*Poor Daddy—they're calling for another day of 100-plus temperatures.*"

*"This weather is especially
hard on Poochie— she keeps
tripping over her tongue."*

*"That's right—a gurgle, a couple of clunks,
a sigh, a cough, and then nothing...."*

(HEAT WAVE)

"Somebody must have asked, 'Is it hot enough for you?' once too often."

"No hug, please. Just a kiss."

"Of course your sheets are all sweaty! My sheets are all sweaty, too! Everybody's sheets are all sweaty!"

"I think you'd better turn it down a notch. The heat just came on."

GRANNY—
THE SITTER

"...and don't worry about the home front—
I'll keep everything strictly under control."

"Now, about dessert—I could make my special orange-coconut cake, _or_ we could just have applesauce."

"As a matter of fact, a vampire and a werewolf are _not_ alike—a vampire can only be killed by driving a stake through the heart. A werewolf, on the other hand...."

(GRANNY—THE SITTER)

"Miss me?" "Can I get back to you Mom? I just passed GO and I didn't get my two hundred dollars yet."

"Poochie likes everybody—but how did you ever make friends with Clara?"

"This is our granny.
She's spoiling us rotten!"

"You're just in time to settle
something. Which is better—
four of a kind or a straight
flush?"

AIRPLANE TRIP

"Lockheed ten-eleven wide-body!"

"I think she just changed her mind about becoming a nurse and saving suffering humanity."

"This is the airplane."

(AIRPLANE TRIP)

"Unisex bathrooms!"

"Don't mention it. We always carry a few for confirmed hamburger addicts."

*"It's really quite simple—
here, I'll explain it to you...."*

"Nice landing."

CHRISTMAS SHOPPING

"Remember now, we're really going to cut down—so, if we stick to our lists and avoid impulse buying...."

"Easy does it,
Dear....Sweetheart,
do you hear me?"

"When _I_ was a kid, all _I_
was allowed was a
dollar-and-a-half a
present!"

(CHRISTMAS SHOPPING)

"Dad's telling Billy the part, again, about how a lot of this stuff is just to look at."

"I'll skip my cousins in Canada if you'll skip your uncle with all those kids by his second wife."

"He's picking up the expensive one...he's crumpling the list...."

"Next year, we'll really cut down—we'll give money!"

OPERATION: SURPRISE

"It's all taken care of—I just told them they were too big to be sneaking around looking for presents, and they agreed."

"I can just see the look on his face the first time he sees this Christmas morning."

"He's opening the trunk...he's looking around...he's reaching in...."

(OPERATION: SURPRISE)

"Wow!"

"You know, Christmas was a whole lot simpler when we all believed in Santa Claus."

"They'll never think of looking out here."

"Remember now, act surprised."

Stan and Jan Berenstain are the bestselling authors
of over fifty books for parents and children,
including the well-loved Berenstain Bears books,
and *How to Teach Your Children About God*
and *How to Teach Your Children About Sex*.